FANTASTIC!

SandCastle™

Perfect Pets

Handsome
Horses

WASHINGTON SCHOOL
122 SOUTH GARFIELD
MUNDELEIN, IL 60060

Anders Hanson
AUTHOR

C.A. Nobens
ILLUSTRATOR

Consulting Editor, Diane Craig, M.A./Reading Specialist

ABDO
Publishing Company

Published by ABDO Publishing Company, 4940 Viking Drive, Edina, Minnesota 55435.

Printed in the United States.

CREDITS

Edited by: Pam Price

Concept Development: Nancy Tuminelly

Cover and Interior Design and Production: Mighty Media

Photo Credits: Corbis Images, JupiterImages Corporation, Photodisc, ShutterStock

LIBRARY OF CONGRESS CATALOGING-IN-PUBLICATION DATA

Hanson, Anders, 1980-
  Handsome horses / Anders Hanson ; illustrated by C.A. Nobens.
    p. cm. -- (Perfect pets)
  ISBN-13: 978-1-59928-750-8
  ISBN-10: 1-59928-750-1
 1. Horses--Juvenile literature. I. Nobens, C. A., ill. II. Title.
  SF302.H365 2007
  636.1--dc22
                              2006033251

SandCastle™ books are created by a professional team of educators, reading specialists, and content developers around five essential components—phonemic awareness, phonics, vocabulary, text comprehension, and fluency—to assist young readers as they develop reading skills and strategies and increase their general knowledge. All books are written, reviewed, and leveled for guided reading, early reading intervention, and Accelerated Reader® programs for use in shared, guided, and independent reading and writing activities to support a balanced approach to literacy instruction.

SandCastle Level: Transitional

LET US KNOW

SandCastle would like to hear your stories about reading this book. What is your favorite page? Was there something hard that you needed help with? Share the ups and downs of learning to read. We want to hear from you! To get posted on the ABDO Publishing Company Web site, send us e-mail at:

sandcastle@abdopublishing.com

HORSES

Horses are handsome, powerful, intelligent animals. Caring for a horse is a big responsibility.

Jill likes to brush her pony. Brushing keeps her pony's coat clean and healthy.

Amy cleans her horse's hooves every day. She checks for infection and makes sure each horseshoe fits.

Charles feeds his horse an apple for a treat. Horses eat mostly grasses and grains.

Stephanie leads her horse back to the stables. Stabled horses should be let out daily to exercise and graze.

Both Bryan and his horse enjoy their riding lessons. Bryan always wears a helmet when he rides.

A Horse Story

Sara has a handsome horse named Clyde. Mother says he is too wild to ride.

Sara cleans his hooves and brushes his mane. Her father says Clyde can't be tamed.

But Sara can calm
Clyde's wild streak.
Into his ear,
she softly speaks.

19

20

She says, "I love you,
Clyde, for who you are.
Let's take a ride
to someplace far."

Fun facts

The earliest known ancestor of the horse was about eight inches tall.

Horsehair is still used to make bows for stringed instruments such as cellos and violins.

Horseback riding has helped some people recover from mental and physical disabilities.

Horses evolved from animals that had five toes on each foot. Over time, the four outer toes disappeared. That left only a single, middle toe, called a hoof.

Glossary

daily – every day.

graze – to eat growing grass and plants.

infection – disease caused by the presence of bacteria or other germs.

intelligent – having the ability to acquire and use knowledge.

responsibility – a job or duty that must be done.

stable – a building, such as a barn, where animals live and eat . To keep or house in a barn or stable.

streak – a trace or small amount of something.

About SandCastle™

A professional team of educators, reading specialists, and content developers created the SandCastle™ series to support young readers as they develop reading skills and strategies and increase their general knowledge. The SandCastle™ series has four levels that correspond to early literacy development in young children. The levels are provided to help teachers and parents select appropriate books for young readers.

Emerging Readers
(no flags)

Beginning Readers
(1 flag)

Transitional Readers
(2 flags)

Fluent Readers
(3 flags)

These levels are meant only as a guide. All levels are subject to change.

To see a complete list of SandCastle™ books and other nonfiction titles from ABDO Publishing Company, visit www.abdopublishing.com or contact us at:
4940 Viking Drive, Edina, Minnesota 55435 • 1-800-800-1312 • fax: 1-952-831-1632